Get Rich Trading Gold
Gold Trading Strategies Revealed
By Sergiy Buzhylov

Copyright © 2015 by Sergiy Buzhylov.

All rights reserved.

This eBook is licensed for your personal enjoyment only. This eBook may not be re-sold or given away to other people. If you would like to share this book with another person, please purchase an additional copy for each recipient. If you are reading this book and did not purchase it, or it was not purchased for your use only, then please return to your favorite eBook retailer and purchase your own copy. Thank you for respecting the hard work of this author.

RISK DISCLOSURE:

Trading futures markets on a margin carries a high level of risk and may not be suitable for all traders. The leverage can work against you as well as for you. Before deciding to trade futures, you should carefully consider your trading objectives, level of experience and risk tolerance. The possibility exists that you could sustain a loss of some or all your trading capital and therefore you should not trade money that you cannot afford to lose.

For information contact buzhylov@gmail.com

First Edition: July 2015

Contents

Introduction

Short History of Gold

How to Trade Gold and Why

Strategy #1: Gold Suppression Play

Strategy #2: Trend Line Breakout with Moving Average Strategy

Strategy #3: Directional Movement with Moving Average

Strategy #4: Gold Friday Pattern

50 Surprising Facts You Never Knew About Gold

About the Author

Introduction

I remember the day, when working in the office at my day job, developing software; I started to realize that the financial markets, specifically investing and trading are much more appealing to me. Back then, I knew very little about the markets and almost nothing about trading. What excited me was that if I am successful in this business, then I will become financially independent and never have to come to my day job, I would work for myself only. I dreamed of what I would do with my free time. Travelling in different parts of the world, or developing new hobbies were coming to my mind.

On that day, I started my trading journey and never looked back nor doubted that I was on the right track.

I started to trade stocks, stock options and ETFs and traded them a year part time with some gains. Later when I discovered futures and future options I realized how important is to find a market matching your temperament and goals. I had a great success in the spring of 2011 when riding gold and silver mania trading futures and future options.

In couple of months, I tripled my account and started thinking I finally got it! I felt invincible. However, when precious metals started crashing I was caught without a sound exit strategy for my leveraged positions.

I lost some of my gains, but continued my attempts to ride the bull market of precious metals, trading it from the long side only. However, the bull market was over and I lost more. The market was teaching me very expensive lessons in those days…

Now I realize that I was unconsciously incompetent, when I made those huge gains. I was just lucky being in the right market at the right time and leveraging my positions.

I self-studied trading markets for couple of years before I started to make consistent profits. I have read over a hundred trading books and developed hundreds of trading strategies trying to find what works in the markets.

I think becoming a successful trader is a choice, but you have to like it and have a strong belief that you can do it.

The core of this book is four trading strategies that make money for me and can make money for you as well. I disclose full trading rules of those strategies to make them tradable for you. The strategies have been back tested with NinjaTrader software. I highly recommend this application for strategy development and charting. It is free and you can get it from NinjaTrader.com

The book is structured so the chapters do not have to be read in sequential order. You can start reading the book from any chapter you like.

The book starts from the chapter dedicated to the history of gold. I take you on a history journey since gold discovery to our times. I explain concept of "gold as money", the gold standard and how it was applied.

In the next chapter, I will explain how to trade gold and the reasons to trade it. I talk about the choice of financial instruments to trade yellow metal. In addition, I touch on the gold market profile.

The following four chapters are money making gold trading strategies. Choose one that works for you!

In the final chapter, you can find fun facts about gold you probably never knew.

Enjoy!

Sergiy Buzhylov

Short History of Gold

Gold's history is long and complex. When man discovered gold, it symbolized wealth and power. Gold has caused obsession in men and some nations, destroyed some cultures and empowered others.

The ancients valued gold for its rareness, its enduringness and its ornamental attractiveness. Some still believed that gold had magical properties. The Egyptians mined gold before 2000 B.C., and in 1352 B.C., they buried young King Tutankhamen in an exquisite 2,448-pound gold coffin fashioned in his image. See it on Figure 1.

The first large-scale, private issuance of pure gold coins was under King Croesus (560-546 B.C.), the ruler of ancient Lydia, modern-day western Turkey. See the coin on Figure 2.

The Romans issued their first gold coin in 50 B.C., though the aureus, as it was titled (from the Latin for golden), was utilized only sporadically during the republic and did not become Rome's common currency until the era of the Roman emperors that began with the rule of Augustus in 31 B.C.

Figure 1. King Tutankhamun's Funerary Mask, 1327 BC

In the Americas, the pre-Columbian Incas used gold in their art and for décor on virtually everything: Each Incan emperor took his stock of gold with him to his tomb, leaving his successor to amass his own collection.

After Spanish explorers returned with reports of all that decorative Incan gold, the yellow metal fired the imaginations of many in the late Middle Ages. At the turn of the sixteenth century, Spain's Ferdinand and Isabella sent galleons to the New World to find gold, and they returned laden with deposits for the royal treasury, thus inspiring Spain's golden age.

Figure 2. King Croesus gold coin, 540 B.C

In later years, In the United Kingdom, Sir Isaac Newton, warden of the Royal Mint, determined the conversion rate of gold and silver. This helped to ease the big fluctuations in the values of gold coins.

In 1774, the British Parliament introduced the gold standard. The strengths of the currency were determined by the national gold reserves.

In the 18th and early 19th century, other European countries and the United States minted gold and silver coins at the same time. The basis was a fixed conversion rate between these two metals. In France, starting in 1795, the rate was 15:1, meaning that gold has a 15 times higher value than silver.

On June 22, 1816, Great Britain declared gold currency as the official national currency (Lord Liverpool's Act). On May 1, 1821, the convertibility of Pounds Sterling into gold was legally guaranteed. Other countries pegged their currencies to the British Pound, which made it a reserve currency. This happened while the British progressively dominated international finance and trade relations. At the end of the 19th century, the Pound was used for two-thirds of world trade and most foreign exchange reserves were held in this currency.

Between 1810 and 1833, the United States had the de facto silver standard. The gold price was at US$ 19.39 for one ounce of fine gold. In 1834 (Coinage Act of 1834), the government set the gold-silver exchange rate to 16:1 which implemented a genuine gold standard. The American Civil War (1861 – 1865), and Black Friday at the New York Stock Exchange (September 24, 1869), lead to spikes in the gold price of US$ 591.12 and US$ 33.49, resp. per ounce. In 1879, the United States set the gold price to US$ 20.67 and returned to the gold standard. With the "Gold Standard Act" of 1900, gold became an official means of payment.

During wartime, central banks abolished the gold standard to be able to print more paper money, which would help to finance the war. During the 1922 Genoa conference of central banks, a proposition was made to return to a partial gold standard to foster international trade and economic stability. This was only a partial gold standard, as gold stayed in the central banks' vaults. The gold was represented by paper notes.

The uncoordinated return to the gold standard resulted in over- and undervaluation of important currencies and led to the collapse of the new gold standard as a regulation of the international monetary system. Its collapse was prompted by the Bank of England's decision in 1933 to suspend redeeming gold. This meant that citizens were not to receive any more gold in exchange for banknotes.

In 1933, Franklin D. Roosevelt prohibited the possession of gold by private citizens. Gold coins, bars and certificates had to be exchanged for a fixed price of US$ 20.67 per ounce. The only exception was gold for industrial or artistic purposes. The rationale was to prevent the circulation of privately owned gold, which may have become a competing currency. A violation of this prohibition could result into a fine of US$ 100 (or US$ 1,708 in today's values) or 10 years of prison. However, the leading part of the population was unaffected by this prohibition, as citizens still could keep up to five ounces of gold. Roosevelt's prohibition was only abolished 40 years later. On January 31, 1934, the Exchange Stabilization Fund was established and the gold price was set to US$ 35.00 per ounce.

It was clear during the Second World War that a new international system would be needed to replace the Gold Standard after the war ended. The design for it was drawn up during the Bretton Woods Conference in the US in 1944. US political and economic dominance necessitated the dollar being at the center of the system. After the chaos of the inter-war period there was a desire for stability, with fixed exchange rates seen as essential for trade, but also for more flexibility than the traditional Gold Standard had provided. The system drawn up fixed the dollar to gold at the existing parity of US$35 per ounce, while all other currencies had fixed, but adjustable, exchange rates to the dollar. Unlike the classical Gold Standard, capital controls were permitted to enable governments to stimulate their economies without suffering from financial market penalties.

During the Bretton Woods era, the world economy grew rapidly. Keynesian economic policies enabled governments to dampen economic fluctuations, and recessions were generally minor. However, strains started to show in the 1960s.

Figure 3. 2015 1 oz. Gold American Eagle Coin

Persistent, albeit low-level, global inflation made the price of gold too low in real terms. A chronic US trade deficit drained US gold reserves, but there was considerable resistance to the idea of devaluing the dollar against gold; in any event, this would have required agreement among surplus countries to raise their exchange rates against the dollar to bring about the needed adjustment.

Meanwhile, the pace of economic growth meant that the level of international reserves generally became inadequate; the invention of the "Special Drawing Right" (SDR) failed to solve this problem. While capital controls remained, they were considerably weaker by the end of the 1960s than they had been in the early 1950s, raising prospects of capital flight from, or speculation against, currencies that were perceived as weak.

In 1959, the Belgic-American economist Robert Triffin pointed out a flaw in the Bretton Woods System. Foreign governments held more dollar reserves than the US central bank had gold reserves. Thus, to maintain liquidity for international trade, more US dollars had to be printed. This, however, would result in a deficit in the United States' balance of payments. Therefore, Triffin suggested creating an artificial currency. This was eventually considered with the special drawing rights.

In 1961 the London Gold Pool was formed. Eight nations pooled their gold reserves to defend the US$35 per ounce peg and prevent the price of gold from moving upwards. This worked for a while, but strains started to emerge. In March of 1968, a two-tier gold market was introduced with a freely floating private market, and official transactions at the fixed parity.

The two-tier system was inherently fragile. The problem of the US deficit remained and intensified. With speculation against the dollar intensifying, other central banks became increasingly reluctant to accept dollars in settlement; and the situation became untenable. Finally, in August 1971, President Nixon announced that the US would end on-demand convertibility of the dollar into gold for the central banks of other nations. The Bretton Woods system collapsed and gold traded freely on the world's markets.

On May 1, 1972, the price of gold jumped to over US $50 per ounce (US $265 inflation adjusted) for the first time after the 1864's Black Friday. In the first quarter of 1973, the currency markets had to be closed for fourteen days, after which the Bretton Woods System was succeeded by a system of flexible conversion rates, without any peg to gold and the dollar.

On May 14, 1973, the gold price broke through the threshold of US$ 100 per ounce (US$ 509 inflation-adjusted). On November 14, 1973, US President Gerald Ford legalized the possession of gold by private citizens. In the next years, many other countries, such as Japan, allowed its citizens to own and trade gold. In 1975, the New York Commodities Exchange was established and trading in gold futures could begin.

In 1976, the International Monetary Fund agreed upon the future of the gold standard and the international currency system. With the Jamaica agreement, the IMF eliminated the pegging of gold to the US dollar and accepted managed floating exchange rates. Since then, currencies are fiat money, not redeemable by gold and theoretically, the money supply is infinitely expandable.

In the 1970s industrial countries experienced stagflation with strong inflation, weak economic growth, low productivity and high unemployment. This decade was characterized by high uncertainty in the financial world, the oil crisis, a strong increase of US national debt, a strong increase in the money supply and a flight of investors into material assets. During this time, the gold price increased 15-fold.

On December 27, 1979, the gold price reached a new high of over US$ 500 per ounce (US$ 1,552 inflation adjusted).

On January 21, 1980, the gold rate at the New York Commodities Exchange stood at US$ 873 (US$ 2,346 inflation adjusted). The reasons were the Iran crisis and the attempted occupation of Afghanistan by the Soviet Union. This all-time high marked the end of an upward-trend and set a record for gold for 28 years.

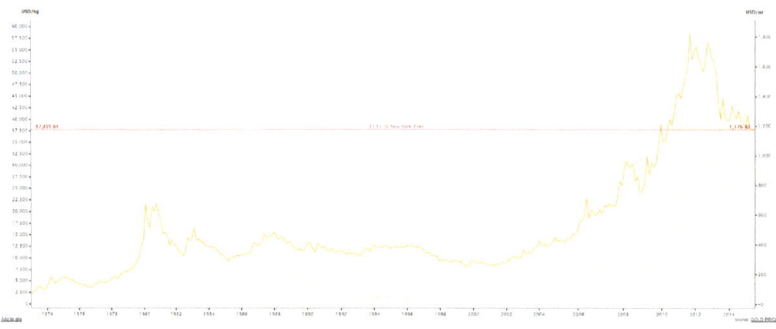

Figure 4. Gold Historical Chart 1973 - Present

In 1980, a 20 year long gold bear market began. To end the economic stagnation, the US Treasury, among other things, limited the increase of money supply. In the short-term, this resulted in a more severe recession and a higher unemployment rate. However, this policy gradually stabilized the economy and controlled inflation. In the 1990s, the United States experienced under Bill Clinton an extended economic upturn (New Economy). In 1994, the New York Commodities Exchange merged with the New York Mercantile Exchange (NYMEX). In 1999, the gold rate in London was at an all-time low of US$ 252.80 (US$ 336 inflation adjusted).

After 1982, China allowed the possession of gold by its citizens. Further, the establishment of the Shanghai Gold Exchange in 2002 expanded considerably the gold trade and thus increased demand for this precious metal. Before that time, gold had to be sold to the Chinese Treasury. Within the next five years, China overtook the United States to become, after India, the second biggest gold buyer.

To regulate gold sales, and thus control the price of gold, 15 European nations signed the Central Bank Gold Agreement, defining how much gold could be sold annually. The limitations were 400 per year or 2000 tons within five years (CBGA1 1999 – 2004). The second agreement, CBGA II (2004 – 2009), restricted gold sales to 500 tons annually. The third agreement, covering the years 2009 until 2014, set gold sales to a yearly 400 tons.

Since 2001, the price of gold has risen steadily. This increase has a clear correlation with the growth of US national debt and the weakening of the US dollar relative to other currencies. In 2005, the price of gold reached US$ 500 for the first time since 1987. Three years later, in 2008, the rate was at more than US$ 1,000. The financial crisis increased the demand for physical gold and exchange traded funds (ETF). The gold reserves of the biggest gold ETF, SPDR Gold Trust, reached 2010 a record of 1320 tons. Therefore, this gold fund controlled more gold than the Chinese National Bank.

In the same year, several central banks planned to ramp up their gold reserves, among others the Chinese National Bank, the Reserve Bank of India and the Central Bank of Russia.

December 2010, the gold price reached a new record of US$ 1431.60 per troy ounce. Compared to gold, the US$ experienced an all-time low. Reasons were uncertainties about a sustainable economic recovery, increasing inflation, possible corporate insolvencies and defaults of corporate bonds. Other drivers of demand for gold were growing national debt, low interest rates and an expansion of the money supply. The decrease of gold production by 10 percent since 2001 and strong demand for jewelry and by institutional investors were other factors in driving up the value of gold.

On September 6, 2011, during trading session, gold made all time high of US$ 1923.70/oz. Investors were seeing gold again as a safe haven, thanks to the US national debt, the financial crisis in Europe and the fear of a new recession.

June 2015, gold declined from its peak to US$ 1200 and has been moving sideways recently. What will be next?

How to Trade Gold and Why

Gold can be traded via several types of financial instruments. Most common of them are futures and ETFs.

Gold ETFs are a quick and easy way to gain exposure to gold. Shares of ETFs can be bought and sold daily and the funds are backed by physical gold – unlike other exchange-traded commodities, which tend to track futures contracts.

Here are two precious metal exchange-traded funds (ETFs) to consider:

SPDR Gold Shares (GLD)

GLD is the most popular gold ETF. Since its inception on November 18, 2004, it has appreciated 152.93%. However, before getting excited about that performance there are a few things you should know.

GLD did not perform well during the financial crisis. For example, in February 2008, it traded as high as $96.18. In September 2008, it traded as low as $71.34. This is one example of how gold is not always a good hedge against difficult economic times. The reason for the poor performance was a deflationary (not inflationary) environment. Once the Federal Reserve stepped in to prevent deflation, precious metals soared. If we were faced with another deflationary scenario, would the Federal Reserve step up to the plate again? It is possible, but it would not provide a long-term solution.

Finally, GLD comes with a 0.40% expense ratio. This is lower than the average ETF expense ratio of 0.46%, but it still has the potential to eat into your profits.

iShares Gold Trust (IAU)

What immediately makes IAU more appealing than GLD is an expense ratio of 0.25%. If you look at the three-year performance for both GLD and IAU (neither good), you will see they each have had almost exactly the same results. Nevertheless, if you stretch that out to all-time performance, IAU has appreciated 167.74% — slightly better than GLD. Both GLD and IAU are actively traded, which keeps their bid/ask spreads tight.

Another way to trade gold is via futures contract. A gold futures contract is a legally binding agreement for delivery of gold in the future at an agreed-upon price. The contracts are standardized by a futures exchange as to quantity, quality, time and place of delivery. Only the price is variable.

Hedgers use these contracts as a way to manage their price risk on an expected purchase or sale of the physical metal. They also provide speculators with an opportunity to participate in the markets without any physical backing.

There are two different positions that can be taken: A long (buy) position is an obligation to accept delivery of the physical metal, while a short (sell) position is the obligation to make delivery. The great majority of futures contracts are offset prior to the delivery date. For example, this occurs when a trader with a long position initiates a short position in the same contract, effectively eliminating the original long position.

Because futures trade at centralized exchanges, trading futures contracts offers more financial leverage, flexibility and financial integrity than trading the commodities themselves.

Financial leverage is the ability to trade and manage a high market value product with a fraction of the total value. Trading futures contracts is done with performance margin. It requires considerably less capital than the physical market. The leverage provides speculators a higher-risk/higher-return investment.

For example, one futures contract of gold controls 100 troy ounces, or 1 brick of gold. The dollar value of this contract is 100 times the market price for one ounce of gold. If the market is trading at $1200 per ounce, the value of the contract is $120,000 ($1200 x 100 ounces). Based on exchange margin rules, the margin required to control one contract is only $5,891. Therefore, for $5,891, one can control $120,000 worth of gold. As a trader, this gives you the ability to leverage $1 to control roughly $20.

When choosing between futures and ETFs to trade gold consider if you need the leverage that futures provide. Futures let you make much bigger profits if your strategy is profitable. But they also increase your per-trade risk and may lead to large losses if your strategy goes south. The leverage is called a double-edged sword for a reason.

I choose to trade futures because I trade only strategies that I am confident about. I know that in a series of trades (at least 10) there is a very good probability that I will make money. Then if so, I want to leverage my profit. If a strategy starts performing poorly, I simply stop trading it, readjust it for the current market condition or replace it with a new strategy.

Another advantage of trading gold futures is that they are available to trade almost 24 hours 5 days a week. Therefore, you can choose a time when it is convenient for you to trade them. This is important in case you have a day job and only trade part-time.

Below is the gold futures contract specification:

Gold Futures Contract (GC)

Exchange: NYMEX
Trading Hours (EST): Sunday – Friday 6:00 p.m. – 5:15 p.m.
Contract Size: 100 troy ounces
Minimum Fluctuation (tick size): $0.10 per troy ounce
Settlement Type: Physical

There are two smaller size gold contracts traded in NYMEX exchange: miNY Gold (QO) and E-micro Gold (MGC) with contract sizes of 50 and 10 troy ounces respectively. However, these contracts are traded with much less volume.

With all this information above about gold, what is so special about it and why trading it? I will explain why I chose to trade it and maybe you, my reader, will chose it too.

Figure 5. NYMEX Trading Floor

First, gold is trending market in all time frames (daily, hours and minutes charts). Biggest money you can make by catching a good trend. I will explain how to do it in the later chapters of this book dedicated to trading strategies.

Second, gold is a boom/bust market when there is a fear in the markets that can be caused by instability (war) in the world or financial crisis when people lose confidence in paper money. It is obvious when such events occur so the gold movement in these situations can be predicted, therefore you can profit from it.

Third, gold is a manipulated market to some extent. Those manipulations have a certain known profile. Once it is studied, it can be arbitraged for a profit. Look at my Suppression Play strategy for details.

Strategy #1: Gold Suppression Play

The major London gold dealers, in 1919, decided to get together in the offices of N.M. Rothschild to "fix" the price of gold each day. The "Gold Fixing" era had begun. While this was notionally with the intention of setting the clearing price at which all buying interest and all selling interest balanced, the possibility for market manipulation and self-dealing is inherently systemic in such a cozy arrangement. This quaint anti-competitive procedure continues to this day. In no other market in the world do the major players get together each day and decide on a price. Isn't it worth attention?!

Presently, the representatives of four bullion banks, namely HSBC, Scotia Mocatta, Societe Generale and Barclays, conduct the London Gold Fix. The "fix" is no longer conducted in an actual meeting but by conference call.

On November 1st, 1961 a group of eight central banks in the United States and seven European countries agreed to cooperate in maintaining the Bretton Woods System of fixed-rate convertible currencies and attempting to defend a gold price of US$35 per troy ounce by interventions in the London gold market. Those banks started to sell gold into the market with the aim of keeping the gold price suppressed.

The London Gold Pool particularly, was selling into the "fix" to suppress the price and no doubt, the bullion bankers making the "fix" were party to this scheme. This was obvious market manipulation.

In 1968, the London Gold Pool disbanded when it suffered massive outflows of bullion trying to frustrate the free market forces that were manifesting themselves as strong demand for the metal.

After the London Gold Pool ceased to exist, analysis of the gold price data shows quite clearly that the price of gold was heavily suppressed by the exact same mechanism.

The bullion bankers added the AM Fix in 1968. This means there are two times in the day when we know for sure that the gold price is being set in a clandestine procedure that is controlled by just five bullion banks.

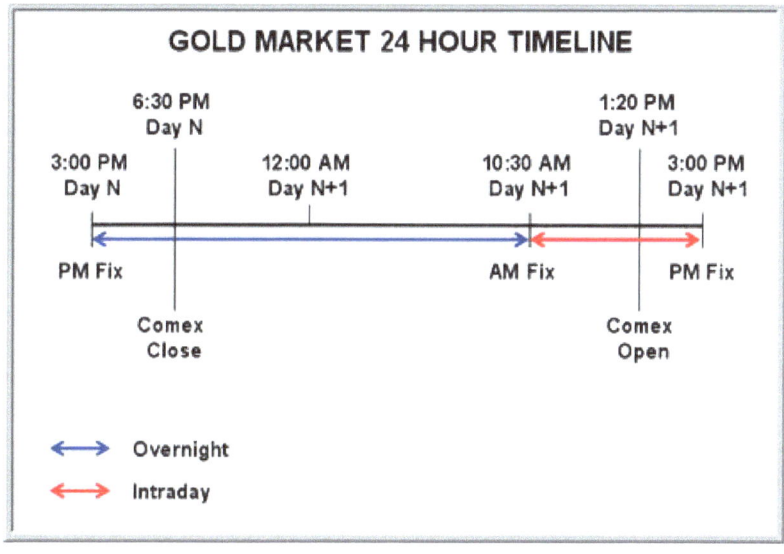

Figure 6. Gold Market 24 Hours Timeline, London time

Let's examine the characteristics of the prices determined by the London Daily Gold Fixings to demonstrate with no doubts that the gold price is suppressed. To do this, let us see what happens in a typical twenty-four hour period as illustrated in Figure 6. We have chosen to start and end the 24-hour period with the PM Fix. Three and a half hours after the PM Fix, the COMEX (Commodity Exchange, Inc., a division of the New York Mercantile Exchange, NYMEX) closes, and gold trading is then predominantly conducted in the eastern hemisphere, where the western bullion banks have much less influence and the market has a much higher proportion of physical metal trading than does London or the COMEX.

The period from the PM Fix to the following AM Fix is labeled "overnight" trading (indicated by the blue double-headed arrow). The period from the AM Fix to the PM Fix has been labeled "intraday" trading (indicated by the red double-headed arrow). The intraday trading includes most of the trading day on the LBMA where 90% of the world's gold trading occurs. It would be fair to say that this is the time of the day most influenced by the western cartel of gold bullion banks. The "overnight" trading is the least influenced by the gold cartel. However, without question the AM Fix and the PM Fix are determined by a process under the direct control of five bullion banks.

Without cherry-picking a sample of the gold fixing price data, I will take the five most recent fixing prices at the time of writing this chapter. See Figure 7.

Date	Gold AM	Gold PM	Intraday Gain/Loss($)	Overnight Gain/Loss($)	Intraday Cummulative Gain/Loss($)	Overnight Cummulative Gain/Loss($)
6/5/2015	1175.9	1164.6				
6/8/2015	1173.4	1172.8	$ -0.60	$ 8.80	$ -0.60	$ 8.80
6/9/2015	1181	1177.4	$ -3.60	$ 8.20	$ -4.20	$ 17.00
6/10/2015	1186	1188.5	$ 2.50	$ 8.60	$ -1.70	$ 25.60
6/11/2015	1180.5	1178.5	$ -2.00	$ -8.00	$ -3.70	$ 17.60
6/12/2015	1179.3	1182.8	$ 3.55	$ 0.75	$ -0.15	$ 18.35
Average			$ -0.03	$ 3.67		

Figure 7. Gold Fixing Data Sample

In this table, Intraday Gain/Loss was calculated by deducting the AM fixed price from the PM fixed price, assuming we buy gold at AM fix and we sell it at PM fix time.

The Overnight Gain/Loss has been calculated by deducting the PM gold price from the AM fix price of the next day, assuming we buy gold at PM fix and we sell it at AM fix time next day.

As you see from the table if we trade gold intraday, buying at the AM fix and selling at the PM fix, we would have a cumulative loss of -$0.15. Average trade of intraday gold trading is -$0.03.

However, if we trade gold overnight, by buying at the PM fix and selling at the AM fix the next day we would have a cumulative gain of $18.35! Average trade of overnight gold trading is $3.67. Isn't this astonishing?!

Figure 8. Cumulative Intraday and Overnight Change in Gold 2001-2010.

In Figure 8, you can see the cumulative intraday change and cumulative overnight change of gold for the period of 2001 – 2010. The cumulative price change between the AM Fix and the PM Fix in this period is negative $500/oz. while from the PM Fix to the AM Fix it is positive $1,400/oz. What this means is that if a trader had, each and every day, purchased gold on the AM Fix and sold it the same day on the PM Fix he would have lost $500/oz. If he had instead bought gold every day on the PM Fix and sold it the following day on the AM Fix he would have made $1400/oz. (these calculations exclude fees and commissions).

Obviously, we could profit even more by shorting gold on the AM Fix, covering the short on the PM Fix, then buying gold on the same PM Fix, and selling it the following morning on the AM Fix and repeated this every day over the same period. Then we would have made $1,900/oz.; a buy and hold strategy by comparison would have gained only $950/oz. ($250/oz. gold price in 2001 to $1200/oz. in 2010).

This demonstrates that the price of gold is manipulated in the market and a trader arbitraging it would have a very good edge.

How exactly the gold is intervened in the futures market, you can see in the Figure 9. In this chart, the average intraday gold price is presented for the last 5 years (2010 – 2015). As you see, gold on average is down between the AM and PM fixes. In addition, it is very noticeable that the price of gold is being suppressed, and sold into the fix times.

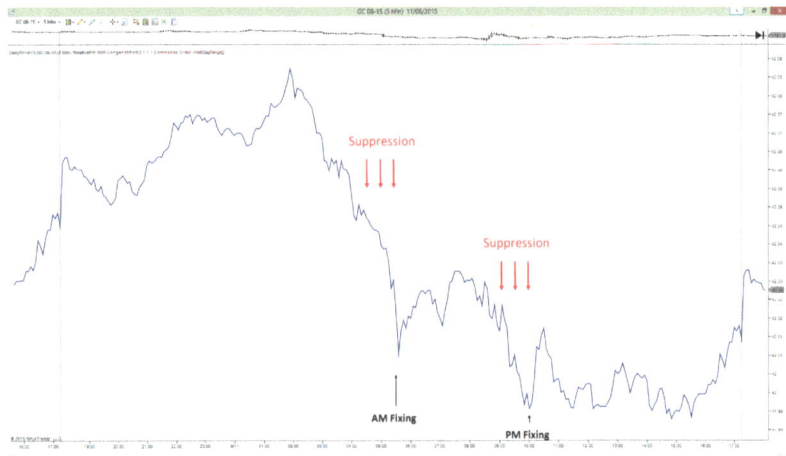

Figure 9. Gold Average Intraday Chart 2010 – 2015. Eastern Time.

So why is gold still being manipulated in the present day?

First, it helps to keep interest rates low: when stock markets are weak, and gold becomes unattractive by holding its price down, money tends to flow into the stock market.

Second, keeping the price of gold down also helps to keep expectations of inflation in check, which also leads to a lower rate of inflation if savers i.e. companies and private households, react accordingly.

Third, a stronger dollar is another desired effect as gold is the biggest competitor to the dollar as a world reserve currency.

One of the unintentional effects of the gold price interventions, of course, was that they also contributed to the asset market bubble as excess money and low interest rates caused asset price inflation.

Based on this research of the gold price anomaly, I developed a Gold Suppression Play trading strategy.

Gold Suppression Play trading strategy rules:
1. Buy Gold futures contract (GC) at 10:00 AM EST.
2. Close long position and sell Gold futures contract (GC) at 1:55 AM EST.

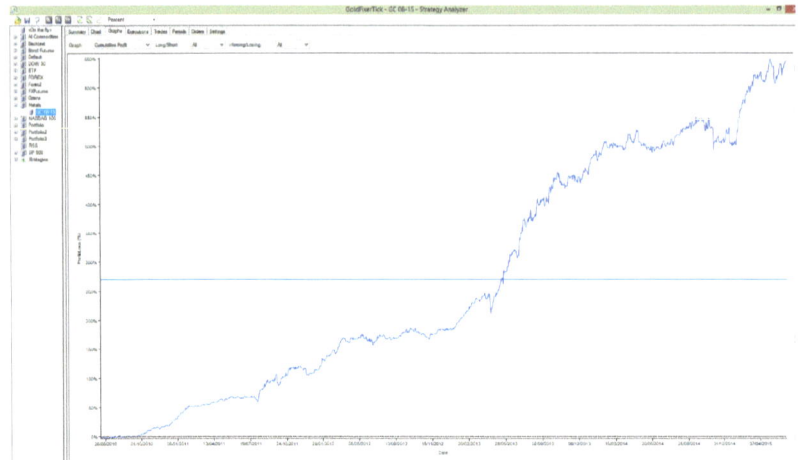

Figure 10. Gold Suppression Play Strategy Cumulative Profit Graph for period 06/13/2010 – 06/13/2015.

Note that in the strategy, the time to go long matches exactly the Gold PM Fix time (3 PM London time). The time to go short has been adjusted for even better strategy performance.

In Figure 10, you can see the Cumulative Profit Graph for this strategy.

The performance of the strategy is impressive, especially considering the strategy has just two parameters: the time to go long and the time to go short!

In Figure 11, you can see the strategy's main performance parameters.

Parameter Name	Value
Instrument	Gold Futures (GC)
Period	06/13/2010 - 06/13/2015
Cummulative Profit	646.98%
Max. Drawdown	-10.39%
Profit Factor	1.37

Figure 11. Gold Suppression Play Strategy Performance Report

Strategy #2: Trend Line Breakout with Moving Average Strategy

Technical analysis are built on the assumption that prices trend. Trend lines are an important tool in technical analysis for both trend identification and confirmation. A trend line is a straight line that connects two or more price points and then extends into the future to act as a line of support or resistance. In a rising market, to draw a trend line, simply connect the swing lows. In a falling market to draw a trend line, connect the swing highs.

In Figure 12, you can see the gold daily chart. As you see, during the periods on the chart where the market makes lower highs, I drew falling trend lines colored red. In addition, I spotted the periods where the market makes higher lows and drew rising trend lines colored in blue.

I added a simple moving average to the chart with a period of 200 bars. This indicator is added to identify the general market trend. If the market is traded above the moving average then we will consider the market is bullish, if it is traded below it, then it is bearish. We need to identify the general trend because we are going to take only a position aligned with the general trend. Therefore, in our chart sample we will consider only long trades as the market is trading above the moving average.

In Figure 12, I displayed four long trades, the buying (going long) entry points with following position exit points.

Let us consider the very first trade at point 1. The market up to that point has been retracing and made three lower highs. I connected these three high points in a falling trend line that is going to act as a resistance line. We are going to anticipate the trend line breakout and if it happens, we will establish a long position. To confirm a trend line breakout, always wait until the candle is closed beyond the trend line, like in our sample at the point 1.

Once we have established a position, we need to protect it with a stop loss. There are two choices here: put a stop loss a tick below closest swing low (stop loss 1 on the chart) or if the stop loss, in this case, exceeds your risk tolerance, you can put stop loss just a tick below the entry candle (stop loss 2). Be cautious when put a tight stop loss as you may often be shaken out from the position on a volatile market move!

Always have a position exit strategy before entering a position. In this strategy when in a position and the market goes your way, in our case rises, we start drawing a rising trend line connecting higher lows along the way. See the rising blue arrow trend line at point 1. Whenever the market closes below this rising trend line, then close the position (point 2).

In four trades displayed on the chart, only a first one will not be profitable (a scratch loss). The other three trades have solid gains.

Figure 12. Trend Line Breakout with Moving Average Strategy Chart

Below I formalize the trading rules of the strategy.

Trend Line Breakout with Moving Average trading strategy rules:

1. **Determine the market trend. If the market trades above a simple moving average of 200 bars then take only long positions, otherwise – only short.**
2. **Draw retracement trend line. If the market is rising, the retracement trend line is falling, therefore draw the line connecting lower highs. If the market is falling, the retracement trend line is rising, draw the line connecting higher lows.**
3. **If the market closes above retracement trend line in a bullish market, go long. If the market closes below retracement trend line in a bearish market, go short.**
4. **Once in a position, set a stop loss a tick below the closest swing low if long, or above the closest swing high if short.**

5. Alternatively, the stop loss can be set a tick below the low of the entry bar if long, or a tick above its high if short.
6. While in a position and the market moves, draw a support trend line connecting swing lows if long, or a resistance trend line connecting swing highs if short.
7. Exit the position if the market closes below the support trend line if long, or the resistance trend line if short.

Strategy #3: Directional Movement with Moving Average

I built my next strategy based on three indicators: Minus Directional Indicator (-DI), Plus Directional Indicator (+DI) and Simple Moving Average. As I mentioned before, gold is a trending market. Therefore, indicators measuring the strength and direction of a trend may be applied to this market.

The Minus Directional Indicator (-DI) and Plus Directional Indicator (+DI) represent a group of directional movement indicators that form a trading system developed by Welles Wilder. The directional movement in these indicators is determined by comparing the difference between two consecutive lows with the difference between the highs.

In general, the bulls have the edge when +DI is greater than -DI, while the bears have the edge when - DI is greater than +DI. Therefore +DI/-DI indicators crossover may be used as a signal indicating that the bulls are taking over, when +DI crosses –DI above or puts the bears in charge when –DI crosses +DI above.

Another signal I get from a crossover of the price and Simple Moving Average (SMA) indicator: When price crosses the SMA up then it is considered a bullish signal. When the price crosses the SMA down then it is considered a bearish signal.

The strategy uses these two crossovers, +DI/-DI and price/SMA, to determine if a trade signal is present. When both crossovers occur simultaneously on the same bar and both in the same direction, then trade is taken in that direction.

Figure 13. Directional Movement with Moving Average Strategy Example Trade

Let's take a look at Figure 13, where an example trade of this strategy is shown. As you see, the strategy took a trade at the beginning of the next bar after the buy signal occurred on the previous bar marked with an arrow on the chart. The marked bar is considered a buy signal because on that bar two bullish crossovers occurred: +DI crossed up –DI and the price crossed up the SMA.

Based on my research, I developed the following strategy rules and selected indicator parameters for the best performance.

Directional Movement with Moving Average Strategy trading rules:
1. **Add following indicators to the daily chart: +DI and –DI with a period parameter of 18 and a SMA with a period parameter of 70.**

2. When +DI/-DI crossover is bullish (+DI crosses –DI up) and the price/SMA crossover is bullish (price crosses SMA up) then take a long position.
3. When +DI/-DI crossover is bearish (+DI crosses –DI down) and the price/SMA crossover is bearish (price crosses SMA down) then take a short position.
4. Set stop loss of 5.5%.
5. The strategy always has a position in the market unless a stop loss has occurred. Therefore, the strategy does not have an exit signal.
6. When in long position and a short signal comes, then exit the long position and enter short.
7. When in short position and a long signal comes, then cover the short position and enter long.

Strategy chart with trades are shown in Figure 14.

Figure 14. Directional Movement with Moving Average Strategy trades

The cumulative profit graph of the strategy for the period of 2005 – 2015 years is shown in Figure 15.

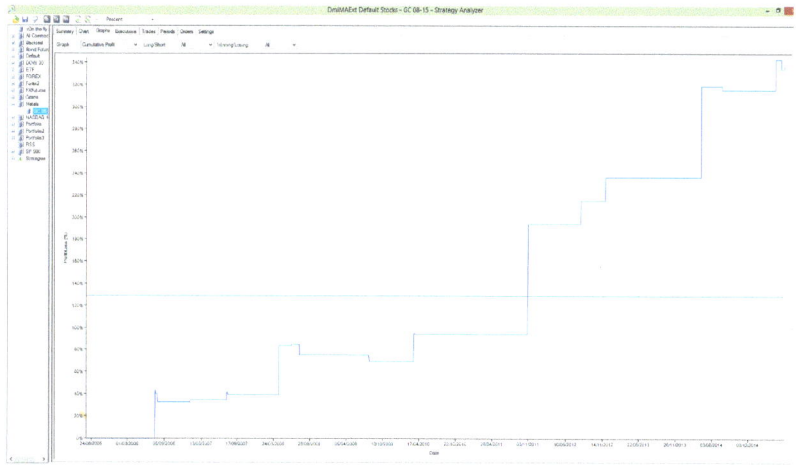

Figure 15. Directional Movement with Moving Average Strategy Cumulative Profit Graph for period 06/13/2010 – 06/13/2015.

Strategy performance report for period 2005 – 2015 can be seen on Figure 16.

Parameter Name	Value
Instrument	Gold Futures (GC)
Period	06/16/2010 - 06/16/2015
Cummulative Profit	337.70%
Max. Drawdown	-8.64%
Profit Factor	10.72

Figure 16. Directional Movement with Moving Average Strategy Performance Report.

Strategy #4: Gold Friday Pattern

Trading strategies based on statistical analysis are based on the assumption that established price patterns have a tendency to repeat themselves. When developing such a strategy we need to make sure that we do statistical analysis on a long enough in-sample period. From another side, the in-sample period has to consist of recent price data. The reason for this is that markets always change, so the patterns do as well.

When I was looking for my trading edges in the gold market, I found that gold not only has a clear intraday price pattern, but has clear weekday patterns as well. My research indicated that the gold weekday patterns could be traded for a profit by taking directional trades on certain weekdays during certain times.

In Figure 17, you can see the gold Friday intraday average price graph for the last year. Do you notice clear patterns that can be exploited for a profit? The price on average gradually falls from session start until around 9:30AM where it makes a session low. Then the price, with two pushes, strongly rises into the session close.

Figure 17. Gold Friday Intraday Average Price Graph for period 06/20/2014 – 06/20/2015

    I analyzed this specific price behavior of gold on Friday and found out that the gold, more often than not, does have a strong bid into a Friday session close. This pattern has been around for years. Based on my research I developed Gold Friday Pattern trading rules.

Gold Friday Pattern Strategy trading rules:
1. **Buy gold futures contract on Friday at 14:15 PM.**
2. **Set trailing stop loss of 0.5%**
3. **Exit trade on Friday session close at 17:15 PM**

Figure 18. Gold Friday Pattern Strategy Trade Example

Figure 19. Gold Friday Pattern Strategy Cumulative Profit Graph for period 06/20/2014 – 06/20/2015

In Figure 18, you can see the strategy trade example. As in any trading strategy, not every trade is going to be profitable. However, this strategy provides you with a trading edge in the gold market.

In Figure 19, the cumulative graph of the Gold Friday Pattern strategy is shown for the recent year.

The strategy performance statistics are displayed in Figure 20.

Parameter Name	Value
Instrument	Gold Futures (GC)
Period	06/20/2014 - 06/20/2015
Cummulative Profit Per Contract	$6,118.00
Max. Drawdown Per Contract	-$439.28
Average Trade	$122.36
Profit Factor	3.83

Figure 20. Gold Friday Pattern Strategy Performance Report

50 Surprising Facts You Never Knew About Gold

In this chapter, I collected interesting facts about the yellow metal that might surprise you! Here they are:

1. You can eat gold … if you really want to. Gourmet shops sell edible gold leaf and flakes that add glitter to everything from pastries to vodka to olive oil. Do not fear for your stomach: The gold is not digested and it just passes right through, according to Edible Gold, a company that sells gold leaf.
2. The chemical symbol for gold is Au, which is derived from the Latin word "aurum", which means "shining dawn".
3. The word "gold" comes from the Old English word "geolu", meaning yellow.
4. Absolutely pure gold is so soft that it can be molded with the hands.
5. The melting point of gold is 2,063 degrees Fahrenheit.
6. There is more steel created per hour than there has been gold dug up throughout history.
7. Gold is very rare compared to diamonds.
8. Around 161,000 tons of gold have been mined by humans.
9. Gold can be found beneath the earth on all seven continents.
10. It is believed that around 80% of Earth's gold is still buried underground.

11. There is an estimated total of 10 billion tons of gold in the world's oceans. That is 25 tons of gold for every cubic mile of seawater.
12. The world's first gold vending machine was unveiled in May 2010. Located in an ultra-luxury hotel in Abu Dhabi, the vending machine itself is covered in 24-carat gold.
13. Most western economies' currencies were on the gold standard until 1961.
14. Switzerland was the last country whose currency was tied to gold. 40% of a Swiss Franc was backed by gold until Switzerland joined the IMF in 1999.
15. Gold is one of the heaviest metals in the world. For example, it is 19.3 times as heavy as water. One cubic meter weights some 19 300 kilograms.
16. According to some, there is enough gold in the Earth's crust to cover the entire land surface knee-deep.
17. Today, Fort Knox holds about 147.3 million ounces.
18. At price of $1205.5 an ounce, the value of all the gold in the world is $6,412,310,567,488 or $958 for each person on the planet.
19. Alchemists believed they could change ordinary materials, such as lead, into gold.
20. A carat was originally a unit of mass based on the carob seed used by ancient merchants.
21. The most expensive gold coin in the world is the 1933 Double Eagle, which was sold at Sotheby's in New York in 2002 for $7.59 million.
22. Elvis Presley owned three cars manufactured by Stutz Motor Company, in which every part that is normally chrome was converted to gold.
23. Former Tyco International CEO Dennis Kozlowski bought a gold-threaded shower curtain worth $6,000.

24. There are 92 naturally occurring elements found in the earth's crust. Gold ranks 58th in rarity.
25. Gold is a great conductor of electricity.
26. Gold is the most malleable and ductile pure metal known to man.
27. An ounce of gold can be beaten into a sheet covering 100 square feet.
28. In 1869, two Australians unearthed the world's largest nugget of gold, the "Welcome Stranger", which measured 10 by 25 inches before it was melted down.
29. The largest nugget still in existence is the "Hand of Faith", found in 1980 in Australia. It is currently on display at the Golden Nugget Casino in Las Vegas.
30. A gold nugget found in the earth can be three to four times as valuable as the gold it contains because of its rareness.
31. The heaviest modern gold bullion coin is Austria's Philharmonic. In 2004, the coin, which has a weight of 1,000 ounces (31.1 kilograms or 69 troy pounds or 828 troy ounces) and a diameter of 15 inches, was dubbed the world's largest gold coin by Guinness World Records.
32. In 2007, Canada made a 100 kilogram (3,217 troy ounce), 0.99999 gold coin with a face value of $1,000,000.
33. Pure gold does not cause skin irritations.
34. Some sufferers of rheumatoid arthritis receive injections of liquid gold to relieve pain.
35. Olympic gold medals were pure gold until 1912.
36. An ounce of gold can be drawn into a wire 60 miles long.
37. Two thirds of the world's gold comes from South Africa.

38. India is the world's largest consumer of gold today.
39. South Asian jewelry is generally more pure than western jewelry, comprised of 22-carat gold rather than 14 carat.
40. Gold is the state mineral of California and Alaska.
41. 90% of the world's gold mining has been done since the discovery of gold at Sutter's Mill in California in 1848.
42. During the California gold rush, some speculators paid more for an ounce of water than they received for an ounce of gold.
43. South Dakota and Nevada produce more gold than any other states.
44. Scientists believe that gold can be found on Mars, Mercury and Venus.
45. The visors of astronauts' helmets are coated in a very thin, transparent layer of gold (.000002 inches) that reduces glare and heat from sunlight.
46. The Aztec word for gold, "teocuitatl", was translated by Europeans as meaning "excrement of the gods".
47. According to the legend of El Dorado (the gilded one), an Andean chief who was covered in gold dust would make offerings of gold into a mountain lake.
48. Evidence suggests that around 5,000 B.C., gold and copper became the first metals to be discovered by man.
49. King Croesus of Lydia created the first pure gold coins in 540 B.C.
50. When Franklin Roosevelt raised the price of gold from $20.67 to $35 in 1934, the dollar immediately lost 40% of its value.

###

Thank you for reading my book. If you enjoyed it, won't you please take a moment to leave me a review at your favorite retailer?
Thanks!

Sergiy Buzhylov

About the Author

Sergiy Buzhylov is a professional trader living in Toronto, Canada. He has a Master's degree in Computer Science. Sergiy specializes in developing automated trading strategies. He has a proven record of making consistent annual gains of 60-70% trading futures with automated and discretionary trading strategies.

References

- Anon. (2010). Facts about gold. www.investinganswers.com
- Adrian Douglas. (2010). Gold Market is not "Fixed", it is Rigged. www.24hgold.com
- Jim Rogers. (2004). Hot Commodities

www.ingramcontent.com/pod-product-compliance
Lightning Source LLC
Chambersburg PA
CBHW040331220526
45473CB00009B/2639